LEVEL
2
AGES 7 AND 8

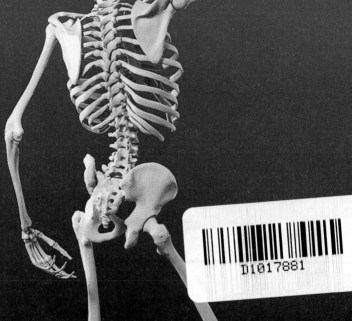

SKELETONS

Lily Wood

SCHOLASTIC
REFERENCE

PHOTO CREDITS: Cover: David A. Wagner/Phototake, New York, NY
Page 1: David A. Wagner/Phototake; 3: Joseph Nettis/Photo Researchers, New York, NY;
4-5: Tracy Frankel/Image Bank, New York, NY; 7: David Young-Wolff/PhotoEdit, Long
Beach, CA; 8-9: Salisbury District Hospital/Science Photo Library/Photo Researchers; 10:
Felicia Martinez/PhotoEdit; 11: CNRI/Phototake; 13: Superstock, Jacksonville, FL; 14:
David Young-Wolff/PhotoEdit; 15, top: James Stevenson/Science Photo Library/Photo
Researchers; 15, bottom: C. James Webb/Phototake; 16: David Young-Wolff/PhotoEdit;
18: CNRI/Phototake; 19: Myrleen Ferguson Cate/PhotoEdit; 21: CNRI/Phototake; 22: Ken
Hayden/Black Star, New York, NY; 23: Ron Mensching/Phototake; 25: CNRI/Phototake;
27: Ron Mensching/Phototake; 28: Terje Rakke/Image Bank; 29: Dave King/ © Dorling
Kindersley, London, England; 31: Timothy Shonnard/Stone, New York, NY; 32: Erich
Schrempp/Photo Researchers; 33: Video Surgery/Photo Researchers; 35: Philip Dowel/©
Dorling Kindersley; 36: Rudi Von Briel/PhotoEdit; 37: Ron Mensching/Phototake; 38:
Astrid & Hanns-Frieder Michler/Science Photo Library/Photo Researchers; 39: Richard
Hutchings/PhotoEdit; 40: David Young-Wolff/PhotoEdit; 43: Myrleen Ferguson
Cate/PhotoEdit; 44: Elena Rooraid/PhotoEdit; 45: David Young-Wolff/PhotoEdit.

Many photos of skeletons show wires, screws, and bolts. These hold together the
bones of skeletons in laboratories and museums. A living skeleton is held together
by ligaments.

Library of Congress Cataloging-in-Publication Data available.

ISBN 0-439-29586-6

Book design by Barbara Balch and Kay Petronio
Photo research by Sarah Longacre

10 9 8 7 6 5 4   03 04

Printed in the U.S.A. 23

First trade printing, August 2001

We are grateful to Francie Alexander, reading specialist, and to
Adele M. Brodkin, Ph.D., developmental psychologist, for their contributions
to the development of this series.

Our thanks also to our science consultants Dr. Caroline Rudnick and
Dr. Candace Corson.

If you had no skeleton, you'd be a blob, like a jellyfish out of water. That's because your skeleton gives you shape. It is a framework, like the poles of a tent or the beams of a building.

Your skeleton is made up of more than 200 bones. Some are longer than a roll of paper towels. Some are shorter than a grain of rice. Bones make it possible for you to move. You could not run, walk, or swim without bones!

Muscles (**muhss**-uhlz) are attached to bones. Bones and muscles work as teams when you swing your arms and move your legs.

Some bones protect your soft insides. A cage of bones called ribs protects your heart. The skull protects your brain and eyes.

Bone is made mainly of **collagen**, calcium, and phosphorus. It also contains magnesium. Calcium, phosphorus, and magnesium are minerals that make bones hard.

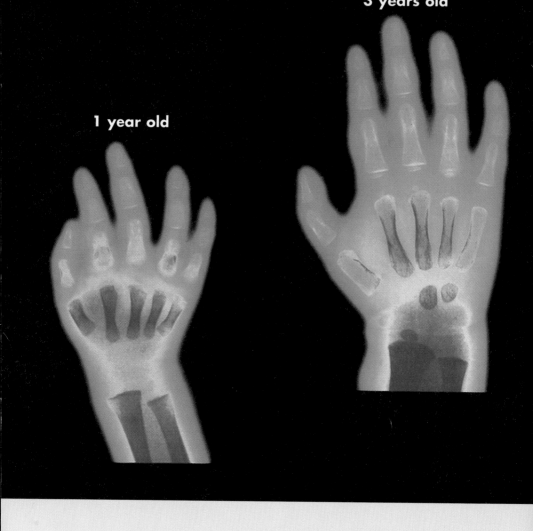

1 year old

3 years old

A newborn baby has almost 300 bones. But an adult has only 206. Do the missing bones disappear? **No!**

8

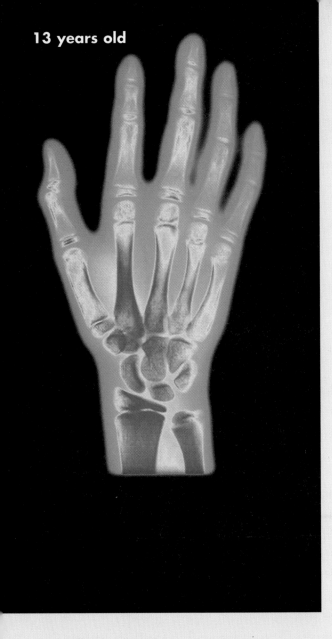

13 years old

This X ray, which has been colored artificially, shows the growth of the bones in the human hand from infant to teenager.

As babies get older, some of their bones fuse, or grow together. Many smaller bones join together to form fewer, larger ones.

9

Take your weight and divide it by five. That's about how much your skeleton weighs. So, if you weigh 50 pounds (22.5 kilograms), your skeleton weighs about 10 pounds (4.5 kilograms). The hard, outer part of bone is **compact bone.** Compact bone is heavy and strong.

The inner part of bone is **spongy bone.** It is lighter, and has lots of spaces, like a sponge. These spaces make bones fairly lightweight. In fact, the total weight of the muscles in your body is more than the weight of your bones!

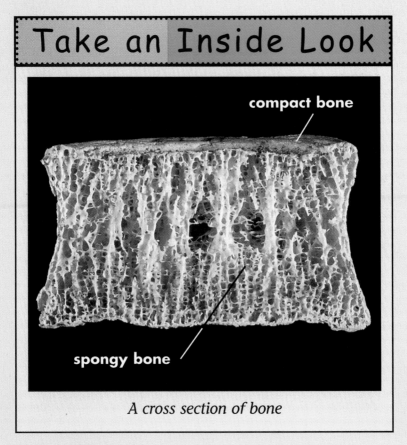

Take an Inside Look

compact bone

spongy bone

A cross section of bone

You may have seen bones in a museum. They are usually dry and white. Living bones inside people are moist. They are brownish or slightly pink.

Living bone is covered by a thin, skin-like membrane that helps bones grow and heal.

Marrow fills the core of long bones, such as arm and leg bones. Marrow is where blood cells are made.

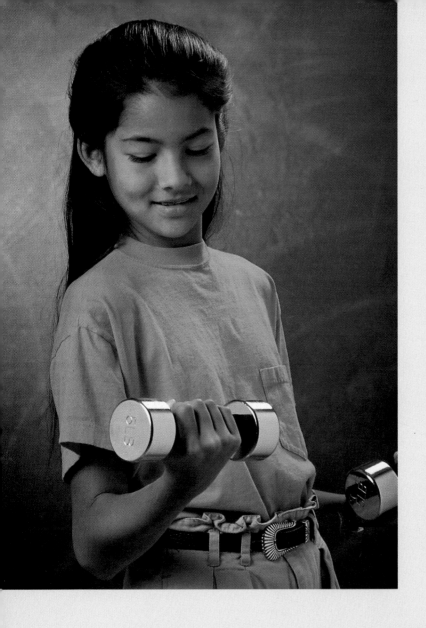

Bones meet at **joints**, such
as shoulder joints, elbow joints,
and hip joints. Joints allow
bones to move.

Ligaments attach one bone to another. Two of the major kinds of joints in your body are hinge joints and ball-and-socket joints.

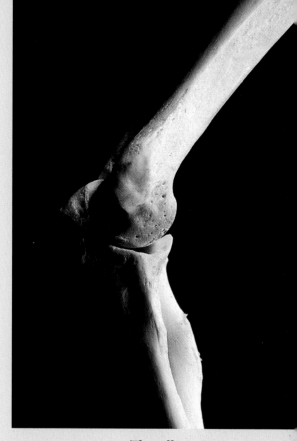

The elbow is a hinge joint.

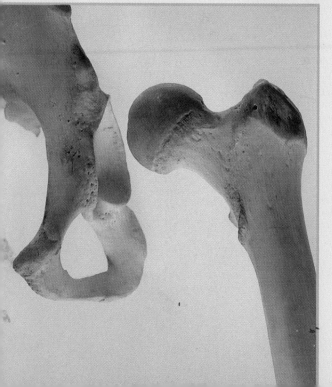

The hip is a ball-and-socket joint.

Hinge joints are like door hinges. They allow bones to swing back and forth, but only in one direction. Your knees, elbows, and fingers have hinge joints. They can bend and straighten, but not too far. The elbows and knees "lock" when straight, giving extra stability.

Shoulders and hips have ball-and-socket joints. The top end of the upper arm bone is rounded, like a ball. It fits into a cup-shaped socket in your shoulder. This kind of joint allows a lot of freedom of movement. It lets you swing your arms in circles.

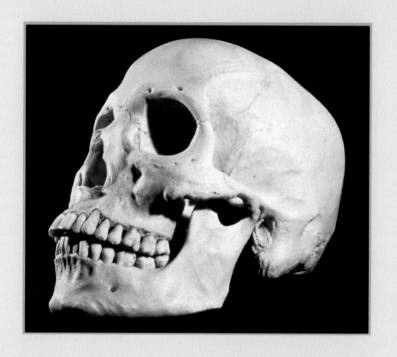

From head to toe, the human body is full of amazing bones. Think about the skull, for example. Skulls may seem scary. But the one you have helps you smile! Muscles attached to the skull help curve your lips.

The skull is also a natural helmet. It protects the brain. The cup-shaped bones of the eye sockets protect the eyes.

The skull is made up of twenty-eight bones. Eight bones cover the brain, making the cranium, or braincase. The face has fourteen bones.

A human skull may look like it is missing the nose. That is because the tip of the human nose is not made of bone. It is made of **cartilage.**

Cartilage is tissue that is softer and more flexible than bone. It also decomposes before the hard, bony skeleton. So a skull usually has a hole where the cartilage was. Your outer ear is made of cartilage, too.

At birth, a baby's skull is not fully formed.

When a baby is born, its skull has soft spots called fontanels (fahn-tuh-**nelz**). These are places where the bone in the skull has not yet grown together. As the baby gets older, these areas will fuse.

Below the skull is the spine, also called the backbone. The spine acts as a rod, supporting your body. It is made up of small bones, called vertebrae (**vur**-tuh-bray).

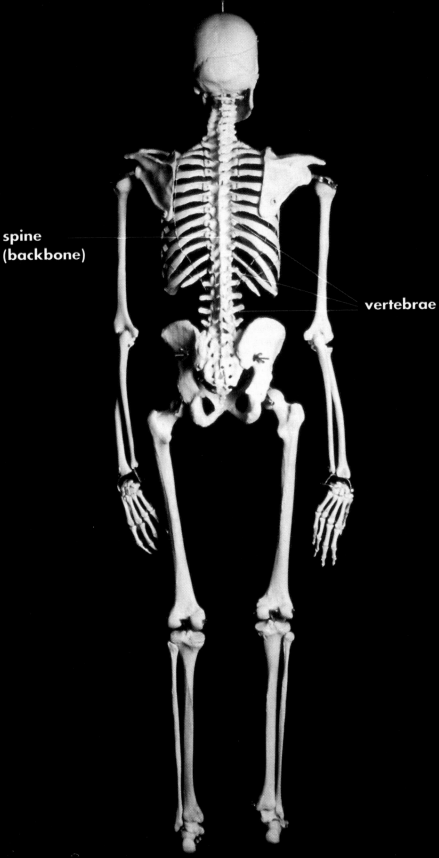

spine
(backbone)

vertebrae

Vertebrae are strung on your spinal cord—a long, ropelike bundle of nerves—like beads on a necklace.

In between the vertebrae are cushions of cartilage called discs. These discs decompose more quickly than bone, so you won't see them on most skeletons.

The human skeleton has thirty-three vertebrae. The lower ones are fused to form the sacrum and the tailbone. Stretching from hip to hip is a bowl-shaped collection of bones called the bony pelvis. It protects the organs in your lower abdomen and pelvis.

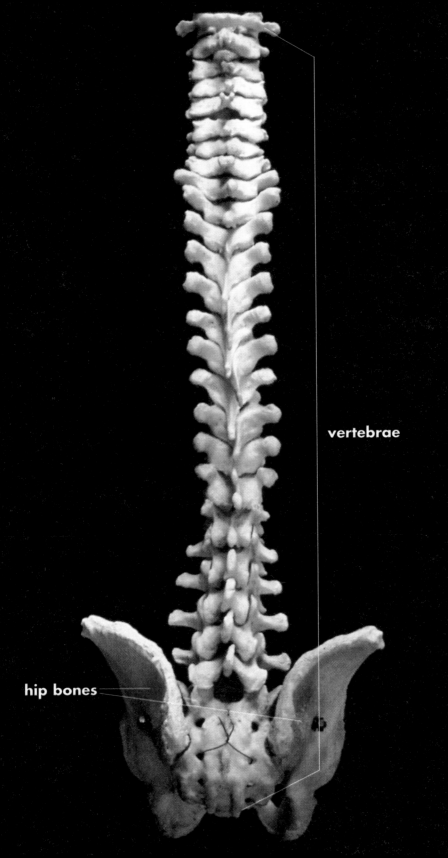

vertebrae

hip bones

Your heart and lungs are
protected by a cage of ribs. Ribs are
narrow bones that curve from your
spine around to the front of your
chest. There, most ribs are attached
to the breastbone with cartilage.
Cartilage allows the ribs to move
as you breathe.

The rib cage is made of twelve
pairs of ribs, in both men and
women. (Once in a while, a baby is
born with an extra pair, or missing
a pair, but this is unusual and
perfectly harmless.)

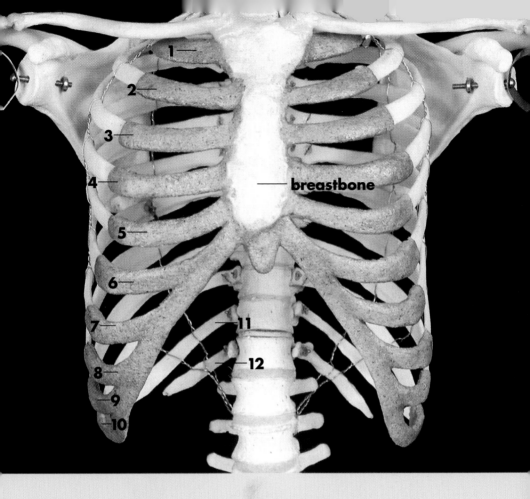

1
2
3
4
5
6
7
8
9
10
11
12
breastbone

The eleventh and twelfth pairs of ribs do not curve around to the front of the chest. These ribs are called "floating ribs" because they do not meet the breastbone.

If you raise your arms, you are
using your scapulas (**ska**-pyoo-luhz).
Scapula is another name for the broad
bone called the shoulder blade. It
connects with your upper arm bone,
called the humerus (**hyoo**-mur-uhss).

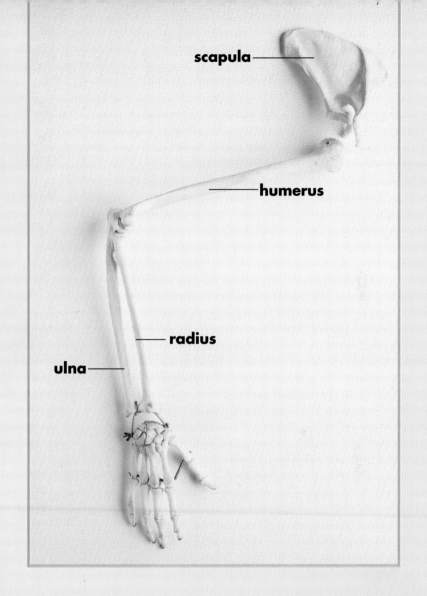

scapula

humerus

radius

ulna

At the elbow, the humerus attaches to two bones: the radius (**ray**-dee-uhss) and the ulna. These two bones make up your forearm. The radius is closer to your thumb.

Hitting your "funny bone" usually isn't funny at all. This area isn't even a separate bone. It is actually the end of the ulna.

The nerve that runs over this area makes hitting it painful. So, you may cry instead of laughing!

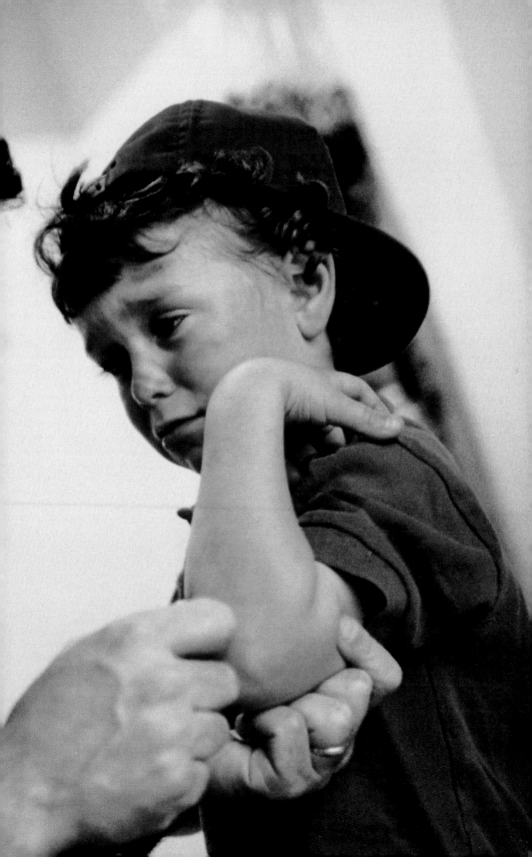

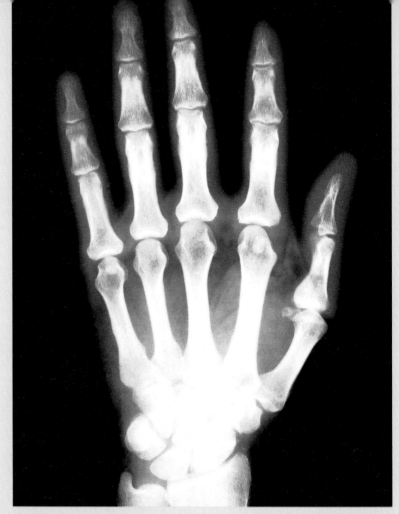

An X ray of a hand

Hands are handy—for playing the piano and doing handstands. The twenty-seven bones of the hand give it flexibility. The fingers and thumb are made of bones called phalanges (fuh-**lan**-jezz).

Metacarpals (met-uh-**car**-pulz) are the long, thin bones of your palm. Eight tiny bones named carpals form the wrist. Each bone shifts slightly when you turn and bend your wrist. Your wrist is flexible and easy to control because it has many movable bones.

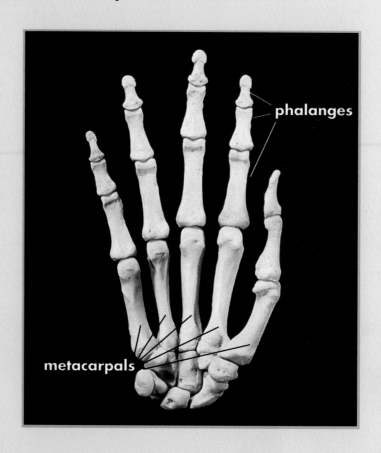

phalanges

metacarpals

The longest, heaviest, strongest bone in your body is the thigh bone, also called the femur (**fee**-mur). It has to be strong. It carries most of your body's weight when you stand or walk or run.

The lower leg is made up of a large bone called the tibia (**ti**-bee-uh) and a thinner bone called the fibula (**fib**-yoo-luh). Like the femur, the tibia carries most of the body's weight. Some muscles attached to the fibula help control the ankle.

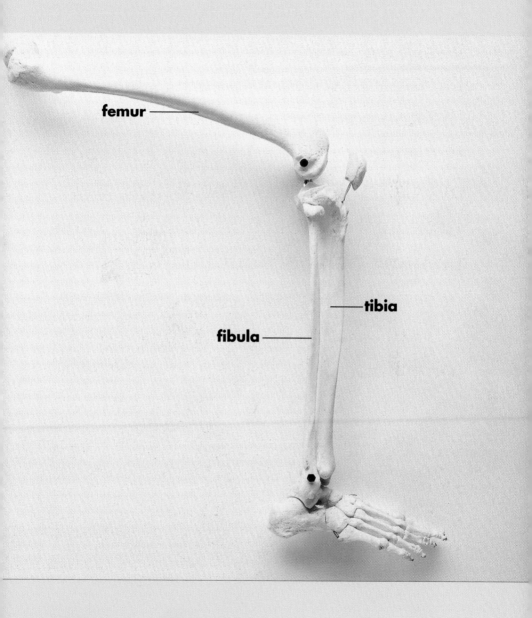

femur

tibia

fibula

On the front of the knee is the kneecap. The kneecap is not connected directly to other bones. Muscles in the leg pull on a **tendon** that slides over the knee as your knee bends and straightens. The kneecap is embedded in this tendon. Tendons, which are strong cords, attach muscles to bones in many parts of your body.

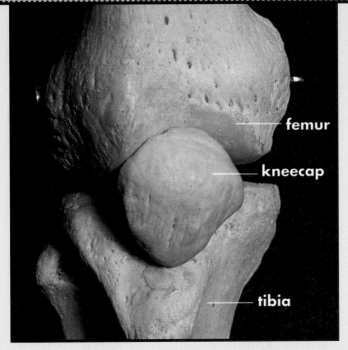

femur

kneecap

tibia

The kneecap is located where the femur and the tibia meet.

The human ankle has seven bones. Like wrist bones, ankle bones can shift, allowing the foot to move in many directions. By the way, the knobby bone on the outside of your ankle is not an "ankle bone." Actually, it is the end of your fibula!

If someone steps on your toes, tell him or her to get off your phalanges. Phalanges are your toe bones. (Finger bones are called phalanges, too.) The human foot, including the ankle, is made up of twenty-six small bones.

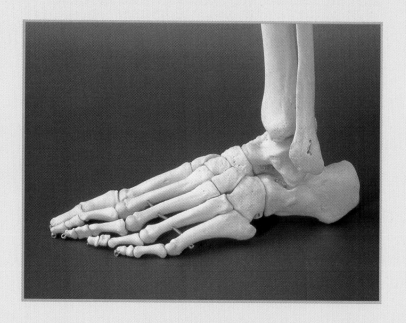

Phalanges have an important
job. They are shock absorbers,
cushioning the weight of the body
at every step. Foot bones also help
you balance when you walk or run.

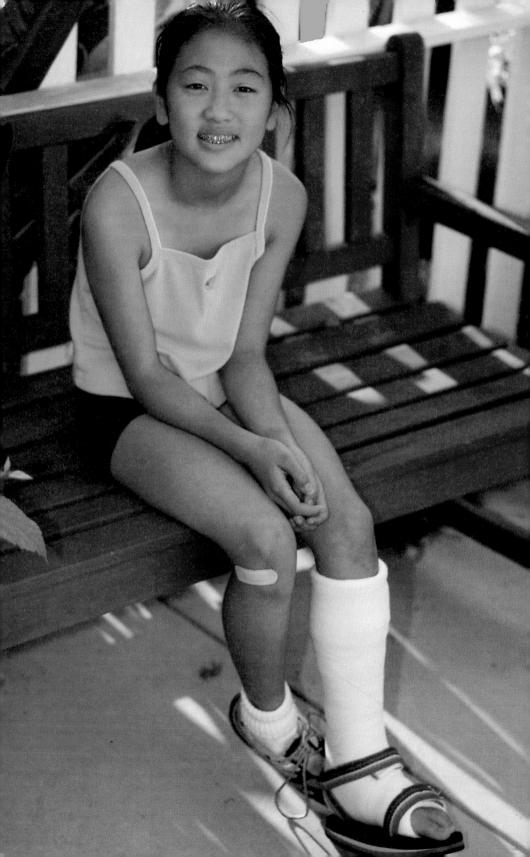

Bones are tough, but they can break, or **fracture**. Fortunately, broken bones can heal. Special cells called **osteoblasts** (**ah**-stee-oh-blasts) move into the broken area and help repair the bone.

How well a bone heals depends on the kind of break. If the broken ends fit together well, a bone may heal quickly. A bone that is crushed or twisted may need to be supported with metal rods or pins to hold it together as it heals.

Bones are amazing. They give us shape and carry our weight. Yet they are light and allow us to move.

Taking care of our bones is important. The key to healthy bones is eating well and exercising.

The human body needs calcium, vitamin D, phosphorus, and magnesium to grow and maintain strong bones. These are found in dark leafy greens, broccoli, milk, cheese, fish, and in vitamin supplements.

Exercise helps build strong bones. As muscles pull on bones, the bones react by growing stronger. That works, whether a person is seven years old— or seventy! So to take care of your bones, keep them moving. If you take care of your bones, they'll take care of you.

Glossary

cartilage—a tough, elastic tissue that makes up the ears and nose, and connects the ribs to the breastbone

collagen—a substance that makes bone and cartilage strong and flexible

compact bone—a type of tissue that forms the hard outside of bones

fracture—a break, such as in a broken bone

joints—places where two or more bones meet

ligaments—the thick, strong tissue that connects bones to one another

marrow—the soft body tissue that fills the core of long bones and makes blood cells

osteoblasts (ah-stee-oh-blasts)—cells that repair old bone and form new bone

skeleton—the structure that supports a body

spongy bone—the light tissue, full of spaces, that is inside bones

tendon—a cord-like tissue that connects muscles to bones

Index

A Note to Parents

Learning to read is such an exciting time in a child's life. You may delight in sharing your favorite fairy tales and picture books with your child.

But don't forget the importance of introducing your child to the world of nonfiction. The ability to read and comprehend factual material will be essential to your child in school, and throughout life. The Scholastic Science Readers™ series was created especially with beginning readers in mind. These books, with their clear texts and beautiful photographs, will help you to share the wonders of science with *your* new reader.

Suggested Activity

Help your child create a model of his or her skeleton using simple materials from around your home. You have probably seen movable skeletons as Halloween decorations, but you can make one no matter what the season! Locate a large piece of thick paper or cardboard. (A broken-apart refrigerator box works well.) Have your child lie down on the cardboard, and trace his or her body with a pencil. Using the information in this book, help your child paint or draw in and label some of his or her major bones. Carefully cut out the main body sections containing these bones: skull, upper arm, lower arm and hand, trunk of the body, upper leg, and lower leg and foot. Use round-head brass fasteners to attach them together at the skeleton's joints.